LIFE-KU

101 Life Coaching TIPS,
17 SYLLABLES at a Time

PHYLLIS LEVINSON

ISBN-10: 0692260897
ISBN 13: 9780692260890
Library of Congress Control Number: 2014913124
Big Tent Books, Gaithersburg , MD

Dedication

To my wonderful husband, Mark, who personifies unconditional love, and to our terrific children, Danielle and Ethan, who are my two most precious gifts. My life is rich beyond my wildest dreams because I get to love you.

Introduction

As a life coach, I have learned a thing or two or, in the case of this book, 101 things, about what makes people tick. We all have our strengths and challenges, our triumphs and setbacks. We have our insecurities and moments of great pride. In other words, we are human, which, by definition, means we are imperfect. So much of our suffering comes from the pointless and impossible pursuit of perfection in one or more areas. Only Mother Nature creates perfection. All other mothers (and fathers) create wonder, which is "perfectly" sufficient.

Life coaching consciously and purposefully moves us toward being as happy, joyful and fulfilled as possible. It is my honor to help people answer the questions we all ponder. "Am I in the right profession for me?" "How do I manage my career and have the personal life I desire?" "How do I deal with a difficult boss/ friend/family member?" "How can I better parent my children?" "What if I'm not as smart as people think I am?" And more. If you have ever thought it, then I have heard it!

My goals in writing this book were twofold. First, I wanted to share the life tools, tips and practices that have helped my clients since I began coaching in 2002. Second, the book had to convey this knowledge and experience with brevity, focus and simplicity. Hence, the haiku format.

Haiku is a Japanese poetry form. Each poem is typically made up of seventeen syllables. In English, these seventeen syllables are divided into three lines. The first and third lines are each five syllables and the second line is seven syllables. Traditional haiku includes a nature reference, which I have chosen to ignore because, well, they are my haiku and I decided to follow one of my tips: if it works for you, keep it, if not, toss it. So I tossed it! I love being in nature but chose to keep the focus on my two goals: to convey life coaching lessons and to do so succinctly.

My hope is that you will read and reread these haiku, and have a flash of insight or a shift in perception. Life change, large or small, is preceded by a change of awareness, the spark of an "aha" moment. Suddenly, we are viewing the world with a new set of eyes; our focus becomes sharper and colors more vivid. I hope that each one of these seventeen syllable life lessons ignites that spark for you.

Phyllis Levinson
September 2014

Acknowledgments

I am very grateful to have such generous, caring people in my life who gave me wonderfully thoughtful comments on drafts of this book. They are all smart and honest – an author's dream team. Big thanks to Larry Bram, Lise Bram, Danielle Johnson Crowley, Danielle Haas, Ethan Haas, Larry Levinson, Cadi Simon and Deborah DeMille Wagman. My dear friend Cadi not only lent her professional editing skills, but her great coaching and listening skills as I talked (and talked and talked) about this book for years. All of these people had a hand in strengthening this book. Thank you, thank you, thank you.

My dear husband, Mark Haas, should get the Nobel Prize in Patience. He good naturedly and happily read hundreds of haiku in my pursuit of choosing the 101 best ones. I am most grateful for his unwavering belief in me and support for all of my endeavors, this book included.

My cup overflows.

Table of Contents

JOURNEY

Life would be boring

If static and unchanging

Transform, change, adapt.

Νo one wants tough times

Yet they're our greatest teachers

Wisdom for next steps.

Living a full life

Requires you to take some risks

Better than regrets.

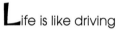

Life is like driving

When lost, you don't just give up

Figure out new route.

Like the stock market

Life has ups, downs and plateaus

Trajectory counts.

Faith is not a plan

Hope is not a strategy

What is your pathway?

CONFIDENCE

What might you become

If you embraced your power?

Go for the brass ring.

Our fear of failure

Keeps us from living our dreams

Fall down? Get back up!

$C$are what others think

About your choices in life?

Waste of energy.

U nsure of ourselves

Even the most confident

Have moments of doubt.

Live large and out loud

Be who you are meant to be

True liberation.

Insecure people

Need to put down other folks

To feel more secure.

$\mathbf{S}$ecure people know

Cheering for others' success

Raises themselves, too.

GRATITUDE

Shelter? Check. Food? Check.

Clothes? Check. Healthcare? Check.
Love? Check.

Cup runneth over.

Sense of gratitude

Is the key ingredient

For a happy life.

See all that you have

Focus on all that is right

Appreciate now.

Look out your window

See rain clouds and naked trees

Warm, dry, truly blessed.

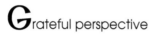Grateful perspective

In midst of difficulty

Makes life easier.

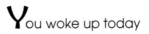You woke up today

Reason enough to say thanks

A new chance at life.

GLITCHES

We think we suffer

Much more than other people

We just don't know them.

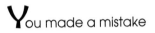
You made a mistake

Welcome to the human race

Learn, correct, move on.

Life threw a curveball

Not sure what is next for you

You'll figure it out.

Instead of asking

"Why did this happen to me?"

Ask "What can I learn?"

Hardships serve us well

If we choose to learn from them

Open up new worlds.

Difficult people

Hard to deal with, be thankful

That you are not them

Overwhelmed by life

Demands and obligations

Put self-care on list.

Annoying people

Are often unhappy, too

Don't absorb their angst.

Tough conversations

Are easier to get through

When you stretch and breathe.

TAKE CHARGE

You have the power

To shift your perspective on

Anything you want.

What would you say if

You had one wish for yourself?

Now make it happen.

If there is a will

There is a way, get going

Set your GPS.

What is your mission?

What is your purpose on earth?

Embrace your calling.

When ninety years old

What will you wish you had done?

Get started today.

Blame game keeps you stuck

Ask for help and make changes

It's your life. Own it.

Life's not black or white

Need to give ourselves options

Many shades of gray.

Be an advocate

For yourself and your beliefs

If not you, then who?

TOOLS

Meditate daily

Calms, lifts, clears, sharpens, opens

There is no downside.

Fresh food, sleep, play, learn

Enjoy nature, exercise

Foundation for life.

Creativity

Is found in everyone

Write, draw, dance, sing... soar!

A good hearty laugh

At least once every day

Dose of happiness.

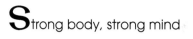Strong body, strong mind

They reinforce each other

Work out both daily.

Words to abolish

"Perfectionism" and "I should"

To be happier.

Feeling low or blue?

Go out and help someone else

A great pick-me-up.

RELATIONSHIPS

Home should be respite

From work, school, obligations

Need soft place to land.

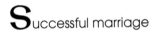

Successful marriage

Must include shared values and

Mutual respect.

True friends have your back

No matter the circumstance

They're life's precious gems.

White lies are still lies

Relationships must have trust

Crumble without it.

Alone is better

Than to be with anyone

Who's not right for you.

Choose friends carefully

Hopeful, positive people

Will energize you.

Same types of people

Keep showing up in your life

Not coincidence.

"**Y**ou complete me" myth

Only true in the movies

Must complete yourself.

Other animals

Feel love, joy and compassion

They deserve respect.

PARENTING

Children soar when have

True unconditional love

It's free and easy.

Guiding your children

Is not same as molding them

Into your image.

Once you're a parent

Your heart is theirs forever.

Wonderful and hard.

Those annoying quirks

That appear in your partner

Show up in your kids!

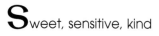

Sweet, sensitive, kind

Strong, determined, powerful

Gender neutral traits.

Parenting requires

Moments of just hanging out

Chill, relax, enjoy.

Close relationships

With your future adult kids

Starts when they are young.

Happy and healthy

My mother's wish for her kids

I have become her.

Goal of parenting

Work yourself out of a job

Guide them to take flight.

SELF-IMAGE

Feel inadequate

Too fat, thin, short, tall, bald, old

Social messaging.

Superwoman. Ugh.

No such thing, does not exist.

Change the narrative.

Design your Barbie

Five feet four, thirty-plus waist

Average woman.

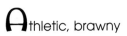 Athletic, brawny

Masculine stereotype

Pressure on boys, men.

Even top models

Don't look like top models look

After airbrushing.

 Different standards

Men look dashing, women worn

Sexism as we age.

COMPASSION

True compassion is

Seeing other people as

Our mirror image.

Teach children to care

About who and what exists

Beyond their own home.

There is no "other"

We're all in this together

This thing called living.

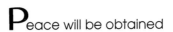Peace will be obtained

When compassion becomes our

Shared belief system.

Care more for others

If you want to feel better

About yourself, too.

Best comedians

Funny without being mean

We should do the same.

Just live and let live

So difficult for humans

Judgmental species.

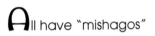All have "mishagos"

Yiddish word for "craziness"

Forgiveness is key.

Compassion for all

Must include all animals

Not only humans.

PRESENCE AND INSIGHT

Rush, rush, rush, rush, rush

Rush, rush, rush, rush, rush, rush, rush

You're missing your life.

When unsure of self

Stop checking above your neck

Listen to your gut.

When is good enough

Good enough? When do you choose

To enjoy yourself?

More, bigger, better

Wanting, longing, yearning for

Missing out on now.

Feeling overwhelmed

Is your signal to slow down

And gain perspective.

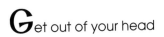et out of your head

Get acquainted with your heart

That's where the truth lies.

Deep down inside you

Are your real desires and wants

Be still and listen.

SIMPLIFY

Life can be simpler

If we remember three things

Love, laugh, be healthy.

Don't get sucked into

Obligations that aren't yours

Keep your focus sharp.

Life lessons from dog

Give love, enjoy treats, take walk

Ahhh... the perfect day.

We have too much stuff.

Do you want a clear, sharp mind?

Toss, donate, be free.

Organize yourself

Everything has a place

Feel better, save time.

It's hard to focus

When life gets complicated

Quiet down the noise.

AGING

Another birthday

Shines spotlight on living life

With meaning, purpose.

Do not fear aging

Wisdom acquired compensates

For wrinkles, sagging.

Wake up! Some day's here

Future became the present

Ahh... turning fifty.

Spring ahead, Fall back

Time to change the clocks again

Life is whooshing by.

Cut, slice and inject

To erase signs of aging

At war with ourselves.

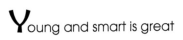Young and smart is great

Experience is better

Can't be found in books.

LOVE AND JOY

Old self to young self:

Life's all about love and peace

The rest is filler.

Half-full or half-empty

Is the difference between

Joy or depression.

More lessons from dog

Love, sleep, eat, stretch, walk, run, love

Always back to love.

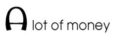 lot of money

Buys leisure and luxuries

Just not love or joy.

"I love you" is nice

But acts of love are better

Say it AND do it.

The Beatles were right

Simple lyrics, true message

All you need is love.

About the Author

Life and executive coach Phyllis Levinson, PCC is in the life-changing business, with clients and speaking engagements throughout the United States. Her speaking topics range from the truths and myths of life balance to the keys for attaining career success for women and minorities.

Before becoming a certified coach in 2002, Levinson worked in both for-profit and not-for-profit organizations, and she understands the challenges and opportunities encountered by leaders at all levels. She holds degrees from the University of Connecticut and Harvard University. Find out more about her coaching and speaking at www.bigtentcoaching.com.

When not coaching, speaking, or writing, Levinson spends her time as an animal rights activist, political advocate, crafter, and Sudoku buff. Her greatest joy is sitting around the dining room table talking and laughing with her husband and children while the nonhumans walk, run, bark, chirp, and fly all around.

Levinson and her husband live in Maryland.

34376957R00084

Made in the USA
Middletown, DE
21 August 2016